His Touch Is Love

His Touch Is Love

Fay Blix Van Dyk

Southern Publishing Association
Nashville, Tennessee

This book was
Edited by Gerald Wheeler
Designed by Mark O'Connor
Cover design by Bob Redden
Cover photo by Dave Damer

Type set: 11/13 Souvenir

Printed in U.S.A.

Library of Congress Cataloging in Publication Data

Van Dyk, Fay Blix, 1951-
His touch is love.

1. Jesus Christ—Biography. 2. Christian biography—Palestine. I. Title.
BT301.2.V35 232.9'01 78-6523
ISBN 0-8127-0189-5

Dedicated to

the memory of Marion Swanepoel, whose tender human touch gave me one of my clearest glimpses of the Divine.

Acknowledgments

A book represents what can happen when supportive, caring people surround its author. It necessarily inspires many spontaneous thank yous. Mine is no exception.

First of all, I'd like to say thank you to the women of the residence halls of Walla Walla College for serving as my guinea pigs. All of the material in my book I used in dormitory worships. The feedback I received encouraged me to share my thoughts with others.

I'm thankful, too, for people who have believed in me and have shown me their love in incredibly beautiful ways so that their love has helped me bridge the gap to divine love. Special thanks to Dick Nies, Helen Evans, Helen Spechko, and Betty Howard.

Butch, my husband, deserves my gratitude for his quiet, patient support through the rather rocky period of writing. His encouragement has meant a great deal to me. I wish to thank my parents, too, for being the ones who first introduced me to Christ.

Also I would like to express my appreciation to Linda Gage, my dearest friend, for her willingness to listen and to share my ideas, as well as her honesty in her criticism of my work.

To all others who gave their support, I say thank you.

The accounts follow quite closely that of Ellen G. White's *The Desire of Ages.* Much of the conversation is based on The New Testament in Modern English, Revised Edition. Copyright, J. B. Phillips, 1972. Used by permission of The Macmillan Company.

Fay Blix Van Dyk
College Place, Washington

Contents

Introduction

I've known the facts for a long time. Jesus had often been the topic of conversation in our home. We talked about Him so much, in fact, that I seemed almost to suffer a case of overexposure to Him. Over and over again I heard about His sacrifice for me and all that. He'd died for me even though I was a sinner. That was a nice fact to know, but it was just that—a fact. I just couldn't feel beyond that. And I got so tired of dealing with facts. They made God seem so agonizingly remote. I longed to know Him as a person.

And one day I knew I *had* to have Him. He had to become real. So my search began. First I reread the Gospels with one question in mind: How did Jesus treat people? This inevitably led to another question: Would He be willing to treat me like that too? I stumbled across that old familiar quote in *The Desire of Ages*, page 83: "It would be well for us to spend a thoughtful hour each day in contemplation of the life of Christ. We should take it point by point, and let the imagination grasp each scene." When I decided to experiment with the suggestion, my adventure in imagination had begun.

As I studied each encounter that Jesus had with people and tried to relive each situation, I felt impressed with the exquisite sensitivity He had in His contacts with people—*all* people. His methods were versatile, individualistic. He asked the woman at the well to do *Him* a favor; He *touched* the leper to make him clean; He played verbal games with the Canaanite woman; and He invited Himself over for dinner at Zacchaeus' house—different ways for different people, but love always underscored every method.

I have learned to love to watch Him deal with people. Witnessing His love made me become more aware of my dealings with others. "If we gaze even a moment upon the sun in its meridian glory, when we turn away our eyes, the image of the sun will appear in everything upon which we look. Thus it is when we behold Jesus; everything we look upon reflects His image, the Sun of Righteousness. . . . His image is imprinted upon the eye of the soul, and affects every portion of our daily life, softening and subduing our whole nature. By beholding, we are conformed to the divine similitude, even the likeness of Christ. To all with whom we associate we reflect the bright and cheerful beams of His righteousness" (*In Heavenly Places,* p. 54). It has become an exciting thought to me.

As I have conversed with the many women who enter my dormitory each year, I have discovered that they, too, are eager to encounter the *real* Jesus and become like

Him. It is for this reason that I share some of my talks in the hope that my visions of Him might help others discover Him more fully. Because of space I have dealt with only a few of Jesus' experiences with people, the ones that perhaps spoke most to me. I have followed Him throughout His ministry. Wherever He went, He left a trail of smiles behind Him.

"Just as we trace the pathway of a stream of water by the line of living green it produces, so Christ could be seen in the deeds of mercy that marked His pathway at every step. Wherever He went health sprang up, and happiness followed wherever He passed" (*Welfare Ministry,* p. 57).

Come, walk with me. Shall we follow Him together?

Chapter 1

He Saved the Day

Mary was frantic. How could she have so grossly miscalculated? But it was true—they had run out of wine. The Jews consider it a terrible shame, the ultimate in inhospitality, for a Jewish wedding to run out of food or drink. Mary, being a relative of the wedding party, served as the wedding reception coordinator. How could she have made such a mistake? She glanced around the room, brilliantly lighted with lamps. The mood was joyful. Friends, relatives, and guests reclined on the comfortable couches and cushions, conversing pleasantly, eagerly gossiping, and meeting with old acquaintances. The young people danced as the older people looked on. All ate heartily and drank freely of the wine. But the wine had run out, and Mary would have to do something about it quickly before the ruler of the feast discovered it.

Eagerly she searched the faces of the crowd for her

Son, Jesus. Surely Jesus could help her—He'd always been so resourceful at home. And deep within her she felt a stirring. Perhaps today He would perform a miracle, perhaps she could reveal the secret to her friends and relatives that she had held in her heart for years. At last she saw Him. The way He looked frightened her a little. She hadn't seen Him for more than two months, and He had changed drastically. The disciples had informed her of His baptism and His experience in the wilderness. John had really put it to her in vivid detail, but not until she saw the face of her Son did she truly feel and understand the hell He had gone through during the past forty days. His face appeared so drawn and haggard that she had hardly recognized Him. She longed to take Him home and fill Him full of her good Nazareth cooking again. But as she looked into His eyes she knew He really hadn't changed—He was still her same loving, devoted Son inside. So she came bursting up to Him. "Jesus, Jesus, we're out of wine!"

His eyes twinkled, and a smile played at the corners of His mouth. "Mother," He teased, "of what concern is that to you or Me?" But His eyes must have said more, for Mary immediately gathered her servants together and said, "Whatever He tells you to do, do it." She had the utmost confidence that He, her beloved Jesus, would come through. It was as if some silent communication had passed between them—as if He had said, "Hey, don't worry. You don't quite understand what's going on, but leave things to Me. I'll settle them in My own way." Yet at the same time He made it rather clear to her that she must not interfere with His "Father's business," that it was not yet the time for Him to enter His public ministry.

However, as a tender, dutiful son, He longed to honor His mother's trust in Him. Thus He ordered the servant to fill six stone jars with water, which must have entailed their drawing at least 120 gallons. Then He requested that the servants take the water to the ruler of the feast. After taking one sip, the ruler's face broke into a smile of delighted surprise, and he began to rib the bridegroom: "Most people serve the best wine first, but you have waited until the last to bring out yours."

Mary breathed a sigh of relief and looked on her Son with intense pride. Everyone was excited. Imagine having a person around to keep your provisions in good supply. It was the kind of Messiah they'd been waiting for, one who would meet all their needs. Quickly they searched for Jesus to congratulate Him, to discover His secret. But Jesus, aching because they could not see that He had much more than a bit of grape juice to offer them, suddenly faded into the crowd and vanished.

Jesus' first miracle—rather a simple one—was one He did just to aid His mother and His friends out of an embarrassing situation. However, it says a whole lot to me about the kind of person Jesus is. He cares about human happiness, the simple joys of life, and He's willing to help us out of our silliest goofs just to save us from embarrassment. I like that.

Chapter 2

A Midnight Encounter

As he made his way to the Mount of Olives he looked cautiously about and behind to make sure no one followed him. It was one time he did not want anyone to see him. After all, what would happen if it ever got out that he, Dr. Nicodemus, Pharisee, member of the Sanhedrin, great teacher in Israel, had sought a private interview with Jesus, a new upstart who was an unrecognized, unofficial rabbi from Galilee. The Sanhedrin would scorn him and ridicule him mercilessly. He couldn't take the risk of embarrassment; so he arranged to come at night when darkness would shroud his activities. But he still felt uneasy.

If I had been Jesus, I think I would have told him to go discuss his problems with someone else. Probably I would have said, "If you are too proud to associate with me—if you're too ashamed to let anyone see you with me—then you can just forget it." Or I might have insisted that we have our interview in a less-secluded spot. But Jesus didn't worry about things like that. Jesus cooperated with his desires, consented to a nightly interview, and tried to meet his needs. Not caring what others thought of Him, He accepted Nicodemus on his own terms.

But, even though he was highly educated and had had plenty of experience teaching in Israel, Nicodemus felt rather timid as he came into the presence of Jesus. That was strange, for Jesus was simply a humble Galilean and had no formal education or authorization as a teacher. Yet something about Him commanded respect.

Nicodemus began the conversation by complimenting Jesus: "Rabbi, . . . we realize that You are a teacher who has come from God. For no one could show the signs that You show unless God were with Him." Nicodemus attempted to get the discussion off the ground by talking about Jesus' identity. It must have been a tempting topic for Jesus. Most of us love to discuss our identities. But Jesus, in His typical, sensitive way, saw that it was only a means to pave the way for discussing deeper issues. He recognized Nicodemus as a seeker after truth, anxious to get to the point, but afraid to do so too quickly. Jesus saved Nicodemus the torture of opening trivialities and went directly to the object of Nicodemus' search.

"Believe Me, a man cannot see the kingdom of God without being born again."

Startled, Nicodemus hadn't expected the conversation to swing that way so rapidly, and it caught him off guard. Born again—the concept was not unusual to him—non-Jews always had to be adopted to become sons of Abraham. But the idea of a regular Jew's having to be born again curdled his stomach. His religion had taught him that being a son of Abraham was a passport to the kingdom. Could it be that he, Dr. Nicodemus, needed rebirth in order to gain salvation? The thought disturbed him greatly. His defenses aroused, he triggered back the question, "How can a man who has grown old possibly be born? Surely he cannot go into his mother's womb a second time to be born."

But Jesus didn't argue back. Instead He simply repeated His declaration and illustrated His point. As they sat on the wooded hillside in the still of the night, they could hear the breezes swish softly through the trees. "Listen," Jesus said; "listen to the wind." They paused. "Where does it come from? Where is it going? You can hear the wind and see its results, but that's about all you can know about it. Well, that's the way it is with the Spirit of God. You can't tell how a man is born by the wind of the Spirit."

"How on earth can things like this happen?" Nicodemus inquired.

"Aren't you that famous teacher in Israel that I keep hearing about?" Jesus asked playfully. "And you do not recognize these things? These things are elementary." His voice contained a note of kindness. Then—in spite of the fact that the proud Pharisee who had been embarrassed to be seen with Him had proved himself ignorant about the things he should have taught the people of Israel—Jesus began to patiently outline the essentials necessary for salvation. Step by step Jesus explained the process. Never again in all His earthly ministry did He explain salvation in such detail and with such clarity.

During the conversation Jesus revealed His mission. To Nicodemus, the ruler of the Sanhedrin who scorned to be classed with Him, Jesus first told about His crucifixion. It was a tremendous secret to share with someone so unworthy. But Jesus didn't view things that way, for in Nicodemus, cautious though the man was, Jesus saw an invaluable ally. With Nicodemus He shared that beautiful saying memorialized through time: "For God so loved the world, that he gave his only begotten Son, that whosoever believeth in him should not perish, but have everlasting life." That night Jesus taught Nicodemus one of the most beautiful lessons in all history.

But Nicodemus did not respond immediately to what Jesus had said. He left that night without making any sort of commitment, but his mind whirled with the thoughts that Jesus had implanted in his brain. In the weeks and months that followed, Nicodemus spent much time trying to determine whether the things Jesus had shared were true. And his study was not in vain. Often in the Sanhedrin when the rulers responded in jealous, passionate anger to some of the unconventional things Jesus did, Nicodemus would calmly urge a course of caution and restraint. Repeatedly he thwarted the devious plans of the priests to eliminate Jesus.

Although Nicodemus did not come out in open support of Jesus before His crucifixion, he certainly contributed to Jesus' ministry by being an effective, though subtle, ally. Jesus didn't hound Nicodemus either. He didn't sit on his doorstep every day and say, "Have you accepted Jesus Christ as your personal Saviour yet?" No—Jesus left him alone to think and to watch, for He knew that Nicodemus needed time to make a decision.

And Nicodemus took time. The whole thing jelled for him the day of the Crucifixion. His mind filled with consternation because neither he nor Gamaliel had received a summons to the trial proceedings that had condemned Jesus to death. He had rushed out to Calvary only to see Jesus already hanging on a cross. As he saw Him there his mind flashed back to the conversation the two of them had had together that night so long ago. He remembered Jesus saying, "The Son of Man must be lifted above the heads of men—as Moses lifted up that serpent in the desert—so that everyone who believes in him . . . should have eternal life." And now he knew—here was the Christ. The Crucifixion had made the difference. It had proved to him Christ's divinity. Ironically the event which had plunged the disciples into the depths of despair and fear caused Nicodemus to make his decision for Christ and gave him hope.

From that moment onward Nicodemus was an avid and open follower of Jesus. Together with Joseph of Arimathea he approached Pilate and asked for the body of Jesus. Tenderly, with their own hands they removed Jesus from the cross. Nicodemus had brought over a hundred pounds of expensive embalming spices, and Joseph provided a new tomb. Jesus received the burial of a prince or a ruler of the Sanhedrin.

Immediately Nicodemus came to the aid of Jesus' disciples. Risking his title, his fortune, and his reputation, he aligned himself completely with Christ's cause. Unstintingly he gave of his vast wealth to the early church. He willingly sacrificed all, because one night he had encountered Jesus. One night Jesus had accepted him on his own terms and explained gently but explicitly just what he needed to know.

Chapter 3

One Day at the Well

She made her way to Jacob's well about noon. By drawing water at that time of the day she could avoid those who labeled her an outcast, for most people came to get their water either early in the morning or in the cool of the evening. Today, however, to her surprise she noticed someone sitting at the well.

As she drew nearer she noticed that the intruder was a Jew. She spat on the ground. Jews—the very sight of them made her blood boil. The racial hatred between her people, the Samaritans, and the Jews was so intense that they would go to great lengths to avoid any sort of social interchange. When traveling to Galilee, Jews would go miles out of their way to avoid passing through Samaria. The two groups despised each other. She ignored Him and began to draw water.

Suddenly He spoke. "Please give Me a drink."

Flabbergasted, she almost dropped her waterpot. A Jew asking a favor of a Samaritan? Incredible! But more than that—He was a man. Men just didn't talk to women in public. One of the basic Jewish laws stated, "Let no one talk with a woman in the street, no, not with his own wife." Most Jewish men wouldn't even allow women to count change into their hands for fear of contamination. Yet here He was—a man, a Jew—asking a favor of her—a woman and a Samaritan. And it was one she couldn't refuse to give either. No Oriental would think of withholding a drink of water from a thirsty traveler, regardless of his race. It was a sacred duty. Her curiosity completely aroused, she forgot herself. "How can You, a Jew, ask for a drink from me, a woman of Samaria?"

He smiled. "If you knew what God can give, and if you knew who it is that said to you, 'Give Me a drink,' you would have asked Him, and He would have given you living water!"

Living water? She'd never heard of the stuff, but it was a curious answer. What was with this man? "Sir, You have no bucket and this well is deep—where can You get Your living water?" she asked. "Are You a greater man than our ancestor, Jacob?"

"Everyone who drinks this water will be thirsty again," He answered. "But whoever drinks the water I will give him will never be thirsty again. For My gift will become a spring in the man himself, welling up into eternal life."

That would be handy, she thought to herself. Just imagine never having to carry water again. But deep inside she had the feeling that He was talking about something more than physical water. However, she continued to play the game. "Sir, give me this water so that I may stop being thirsty—and not have to make this journey to draw water any more!"

"Go and call your husband and then come back here."

She gulped. "I haven't got a husband."

Jesus' eyes gleamed. "You are quite right in saying, 'I haven't got *a* husband,' for you have had *five* husbands and the man you have now is not your husband at all. Yes, you spoke the truth when you said that."

Her mouth fell open. The man was a stranger, yet He knew all the inner secrets of her life. How could He? She felt as though stripped naked before the world. Quickly she started to change the subject before He could reveal any more, continuing with more of her playful banter. "Sir, I can see that You are a prophet." Then she resorted to the age-old trick of getting people involved in religious controversy in order to sidestep the previous revelation. "Now our ancestors worshiped on this hillside, but you Jews say that Jerusalem is the place where men ought to worship." Such friction existed between the Jews and the Samaritans over the proper place of worship that she felt sure her question would put Him off the track.

But Jesus did not let her sidetrack Him into a discussion concerning His status as a prophet or the appropriate place to worship. Instead, He simply made the point that what mattered was not *where* one worshiped but *how*.

She grabbed at another religious straw, "Of course I know that Messiah is coming, You know, the One who is called Christ. When He comes He will make everything plain to us."

At that point Jesus did a special thing. He told the

woman—the immoral, despicable Samaritan—something apparently He had never told anyone else before. He revealed to her, of all people, the greatest secret in all the world. To her He first said, "I am Christ speaking to you now." If I had been Jesus, I'm afraid I would have saved the announcement for one of my closest friends or one of the more important persons in the country—not throw it away on a prostitute. But Jesus didn't operate as I do. Instead, He saw that revealing such a vital secret to a woman with such low self-esteem would make her feel more worthwhile. Jesus recognized that she would not abuse the knowledge as some of the self-righteous Jews might have but would use it to bring others to Him.

And He was correct in His evaluation of her. No sooner did He explain to her that He was the Messiah than she went running back to her village to tell her friends about Him. She left in such a hurry, in fact, that she left her waterpot behind. Bursting into the village square, she exclaimed, "Come out and see the man who told me everything I've ever done! Can this be 'Christ'? "

The people looked at one another in wonder, having never seen her so excited. Until then she had caroused around town, but today she was different. Her entire appearance had changed. The fact that *she* was even talking about a religious subject was enough to arouse their attention. Their curiosity got the better of them, and they followed her outside the village to where Jesus waited.

The Bible says that "many of the Samaritans who came out of that town believed in him." Their salvation came about because one day Jesus cared enough about an individual to forget what people thought. And even though He laid bare her sins, He did not say one word of condemnation. Through it all He made her feel that He was her friend, that He loved her in spite of her past sordid life and was willing to offer her something better. It was love, offered at great risk, that compelled the Samaritan woman to share her discovery with others, making her a better evangelist than the disciples.

Chapter 4

After a Thirty-eight Year Wait . . .

Vacantly he stared into space. It wouldn't be long now—his strength, his hope, were all but gone. He was dreadfully alone—friends had long since given up caring. In years past a couple of them would sit with him, ready to help him to the water in case the angel should pass by. But no one came anymore. In fact, no one had done so in years. Now everyone had forgotten him—he was just another cripple waiting to die.

His twisted limbs ached incessantly. He was one mass of atrophied flesh, a pitiful case of thirty-eight years of inaction. And although all manner of strange and dreadful diseases and deformities surrounded the Pool of Bethesda, those who passed by easily identified his case as the worst one there. They could hardly bear to look at him. Keenly sensing their open revulsion, it made him feel even more helpless and more hopeless. Time and again in the thirty-eight years of his paralysis he had struggled to get to the pool for healing. His heart had filled with hope as the waters stirred. But he had never made it. The stronger, less disabled ones had trampled over him and reached the water before him, and his hopes had turned to bitter disappointment. Hope. Despair. Hope. Despair. It was the story of his life. He could not go on much longer. The pain, the loneliness, the hopelessness, mercilessly took their toll.

But above everything the thought that continually haunted him was that he was shut out from God. He knew he had brought his physical condition on himself. His early life had been one of mindless dissipation, and his paralysis seemed a judgment from God for his previous life-style. Yet he longed for forgiveness, for some assurance from God that he was still one of His children— but he thought that was too much to ask, and he lay on his mat in utter despair.

And Jesus walked by. The scene at Bethesda always got to Him. As He viewed the blind, the lame, the paralytics, waiting in hopeful hopelessness for the superstitious moving of the water, it stirred His heart beyond measure. With every fiber in His being He longed to heal every one of them. But He knew He shouldn't do it on the Sabbath. It would arouse far too much opposition from the Pharisees, causing His ministry more harm than good. But suddenly Jesus' eyes rested on the man crippled for thirty-eight years, and the sight of him filled His heart with so much pity that He just couldn't help Himself. He *had* to heal that man.

Bending tenderly over the old man, Jesus whispered softly, "Do you want to get well again?" The man started—it had been so long since anyone had spoken to him. His eyes focused and refocused. "Do you want to get well again?" Was this man, too, playing cruel games with him? Yet as he looked into the man's face, he saw compassion, concern.

His voice broke as he made one of the saddest, most forlorn statements in all the Bible. "Sir, I haven't anybody to put me into the pool when the water is all stirred up. While I'm trying to get there somebody else gets down into it first."

Now Jesus could have replied, "You fool, you mean after thirty-eight years you still believe in that silly superstition about the angel agitating the water with healing power?" Or He might have said, "Well, I'm sorry, but you're simply having to bear the consequences of your earlier indulgences. That's what happens to the carousing type; that's what happens when you have too many women, too much booze, too much Dr. Pepper. That's what happens when you eat between meals and don't go to bed at night. Serves you right. You shouldn't expect to be healed." Jesus didn't even tell the man of the great power of God or how God could help him. He didn't even require the man's confession of faith.

Rather, He flashed an encouraging smile and said matter-of-factly, "Get up, pick up your bed and walk." Now if I'd been the man, I think I would have laughed. "After thirty-eight years on this mat, you expect *me* to walk *and* carry my bed? You've got to be kidding!" I don't think I would have tried to move an inch. But something in Jesus' tone of voice, something in His face, gave the man hope like he had never had before. In that look the man saw how much Jesus cared. He realized how willing Jesus was to forgive his sins and let the past be *past.* With that realization he *knew* he could walk again.

The Bible says, "At once the man recovered, picked up his bed and began to walk." What an incredible feeling that must have been for the man to walk after thirty-eight years as an invalid. In the same way Jesus bends tenderly over us and whispers softly, "Hey, I'm willing to forget the past if you are. Come on, get up and walk!"

Chapter 5

A Touch That Made the Difference

He was dying by inches. The disease had ravaged his being. Covered with leprosy, the most dreaded disease in all the East, his body was a mass of little ulcerated nodules that continually discharged a foul, repulsive pus. His eyebrows had fallen out. He wheezed horribly. The tendons in his hands had contracted so that his hands looked more like claws than hands. His eyes had taken on a vacant stare. He was, in short, a living corpse.

The people detested him and his kind. They considered leprosy an outward sign of inward sin, a divine judgment. Thus society ostracized lepers. According to the purification laws no one could approach nearer to a leper than six feet, and if the wind was blowing, not within 150 feet. It was illegal to greet a leper in an open place, and lepers could not enter the synagogues. Rather, they had to observe the services through holes in the synagogue walls.

As they passed through populated areas they had to wail, "Unclean!" to warn people of their approach. Considered God's outcasts, lepers lived a painfully lonely existence.

The leper felt deeply his plight. He longed to rejoin his family and his friends. Yet he knew it was impossible—he had fallen under the curse of God. Every moment he ached to know why God had chosen to punish him. It was bad enough to have friends and family reject him, but to have God abandon him caused him to despair. His hope was almost gone, and with a morbid sense of resignation, he prepared himself for death.

But then he heard about Jesus. The whole country rang with news of the radical rabbi. Stories spread quickly about His ability to heal and relieve people of their deformities and diseases. The leper listened to the snatches of conversation he managed to glean at a distance, and his heart stirred. Could Jesus heal a leper too? Could He make him a new man? He hardly dared to let himself think such things, yet somewhere deep within he knew that Jesus could help him if he could only get to Him.

However, it wouldn't be easy to reach Jesus. How could he ever approach near enough to present his request? Crowds of people always surrounded Him. How could a leper possibly work his way through them? Besides, he knew of no record of a leper having been healed since the days of Elisha. Would God be able to forgive him and lift the curse now? Fears of failure haunted his mind, yet hope still flickered.

He decided to risk going to Jesus. The crowd fell back in horror at the leper who failed to keep the distance required of him by law. He was repulsive to look at, and fearing contamination, the people quickly made way for him to approach Jesus. A hush fell over the multitudes as they waited for Jesus' reaction.

The leper knelt at Jesus' feet. In a rasping voice he wheezed, "Sir, if You want to, You can make me clean." His voice was scarcely audible. The crowd waited.

Jesus smiled and stretched out His hand. The crowd gasped as they watched Jesus put His hand on the repulsive leper. They could not comprehend why Jesus would dare to risk touching a man with the dreaded disease of leprosy. Everyone shuddered. But the leper thrilled through and through—it had been so long since he had felt a loving hand. Humanity had shunned and ignored him for so many years, yet this man, this Jesus, was willing to risk all and touch him.

Then Jesus added words to His touch. "Of course, I want to. Be clean!" And immediately the leper became a new man. The scales of diseased skin fell away, and in their place came flesh as soft as a baby's. His eyes lost their vacant stare. He felt a flash of electricity through his being, and he was alive once more.

Words alone could have healed the leper. Yet Jesus, in His typical tender and sensitive way, knew that the leper needed a touch of love.

Chapter 6

Nothing Would Stop Him

Desperately he wanted to see Jesus. If only he could come into His presence, he would die in peace. But would Jesus want to meet him? The thought plagued the mind of the paralytic. His burden of guilt was dreadfully heavy. The thought of separation from God was more than he could stand. If only he could gain reassurance that God had forgiven his sins, then he could tolerate the devastation of the palsy. But without that reassurance he was miserable. The disease was in its final stages. The pallor of death lurked across his face, and one could almost smell decaying flesh. Knowing his condition was the result of his past, sordid life, he was willing to accept the consequences—if only he could know that Jesus still loved him and that God had forgiven him.

Then Jesus came to town. The paralytic trembled at the thought. Desperate though he was to see Jesus, he was also afraid of rejection. How could Jesus possibly accept him after all he had done? Besides, the disease had completely conquered him—of himself he was helpless. Fortunately, however, several of his friends knew of his intense desire to see Jesus. As soon as news reached them that Jesus had arrived, they rushed over to their friend's home. Eagerly they urged the paralytic to make his dream come true. With boisterous tenderness, they carried him on his cot to Peter's house, where Jesus was making His headquarters. But they met large crowds. It was impossible to get through the door. The paralytic grew frantic. How could he be this close to Jesus and not get to see Him? He could hardly contain himself. His friends, too, felt keen disappointment. Obviously no amount of pushing and shoving would make any difference. Jesus was out of their reach.

Suddenly a gleam appeared in the eye of the sick man. Quickly he motioned his friends to pick up his cot, and together they climbed the steps to the roof of Peter's house. Nothing would stop him from seeing Jesus. He whispered his plan to them. With vigor they attacked the roof, tearing up the brushwood and the clay. In just a few minutes they had uncovered a hole in the roof just large enough to admit the paralytic's cot. The crowds watched in amazement. Clay dust flew everywhere, and it was a bit unsettling to see the ceiling dissolve above one's head. The friends borrowed Peter's fishing ropes, and with undaunted determination they slowly lowered the paralytic on his cot to rest in front of Jesus. The people fell back, totally flabbergasted by the gall and nerve of the paralytic and his friends.

Jesus smiled, barely able to hide His amusement at the

ingenuity of the paralytic and his friends. Their faith thrilled Him. With tender sympathy He looked into the paralytic's face. His heart ached as He saw the wreck of humanity before Him. Looking into the eyes of the paralytic, He saw the desperate need for reassurance and for love, and with all the love He had within Him He said affectionately, "My son, your sins are forgiven." The paralytic could hardly believe his ears. His sins were forgiven. *His sins were forgiven!* Immediately his burden vanished, and he could breathe again. Now he knew he could die in peace, and he lay back on his cot in complete contentment.

The scribes gasped. " 'My son, your sins are forgiven!' Why does this man talk such blasphemy? Who can possibly forgive sins but God?" It deeply offended them that Jesus should assume the role of Deity.

Instantly realizing what they thought, Jesus said to them, "Why must you argue like this in your minds? Which do you suppose is easier—to say to a paralyzed man, 'Your sins are forgiven,' or 'Get up, pick up your bed and walk'? But to prove to you that the Son of man has full authority to forgive sins on earth, I say to you,"—He turned to the paralytic—"Get up, pick up your bed, and go home."

The paralytic felt a flash of power convulse his being. He felt life-giving blood pulse through his veins and felt his muscles take on a new elasticity. At once he sprang to his feet, wondering at the newness of his strength, relieved beyond measure that his sins had been forgiven. Then he picked up the cot he had lain on for years and went home. He was so grateful to Jesus for his healing that he was speechless. To think that moments before he had been a helpless man on a cot, and now he was a new man carrying that cot. His sins were forgiven.

Chapter 7

A Call to a Publican

He was a publican but might as well have been a leper. Heathen dogs, publicans—they were one and the same thing. The people considered the tax collectors as flunkies to the Romans, and as such, traitors to Israel. Publicans symbolized the depths to which Israel had fallen under Roman slavery, and the sight of them brought pain and wrenching of the soul. They were the bloodsuckers of the nation. And it was true. Most publicans snapped up every penny they could get, legally or illegally. Their business was an extremely profitable one. Often they were the richest men in town. But their affluence only deepened Jewish hatred. The Jews excommunicated them from the synagogue, considered their money tainted, and refused to accept their testimony in court. *Publican* was simply a synonym for *sinner.* Considered the lowest of society, the publicans were outcasts. And Matthew was one of them.

Matthew sat in the customs office in Capernaum. He did a thriving business, for Capernaum was the chief trading center of the region. His was an important toll station, taxing travelers passing on the main highway from Damascus to the Mediterranean Sea and also the traffic crossing the Sea of Galilee. But tax collecting had lost some of its fascination since the Teacher from Nazareth had begun touring the area. The Teacher had captured Matthew's imagination with all of His miracles and wise sayings, and he longed to know more of Him. In fact (although he was embarrassed because it was so impossible), Matthew had a secret dream of even becoming one of Jesus' disciples. But no rabbi would have anything to do with him, much less allow him to be a disciple, so why should Jesus be any exception? After all, Matthew was a publican. However, while other men saw Matthew only in terms of his profession, Jesus perceived him as a man longing for something better. So one day Jesus stopped by the tollbooth and said, "Follow Me." Flabbergasted, but grateful beyond words, Matthew became Jesus' fifth disciple.

The calling of Matthew to be a disciple of a rabbi greatly upset Capernaum's social circles. The fact that Jesus would accept a foul publican into His inner circle was simply beyond the comprehension of the patriotic Jews. It went against all religious, social, and national customs.

But Matthew considered his call to be so special that he included it in a list of miracles. To him, the fact that Jesus had called him, a despised publican, to be a disciple constituted every bit as much a miracle as healing a man of palsy or raising Jairus' daughter from the dead. He determined to show Jesus his appreciation.

Matthew decided to throw a huge feast in His honor, and he invited all his friends to it so that they too could meet Jesus. Unfortunately, since Matthew was an outcast, the only kind of friends he had were other publicans and prostitutes. When the whole crowd got together, it was obvious that most of them weren't the sort of people one would normally invite to Sabbath School. Jesus certainly risked His reputation by eating with such a rough bunch. It seems to me that it would have been much more expedient for Jesus to have avoided the feast altogether. Perhaps He could have said, "That's OK, Matthew, don't you go to all that trouble to prepare anything for Me. We can eat at the A & W or something. If you want to show your gratitude to Me, why don't you slide a little extra money into the tithe envelope or give a couple more Bible studies to your friends each week?"

But Jesus didn't worry about what people thought. He didn't care if they called Him "publican-lover." What concerned Him was the man Matthew. Matthew offered the best thing he knew to offer—a feast—and because that was Matthew's special way of giving, Jesus accepted it wholeheartedly, even though it practically cost Him His reputation. And Jesus didn't sit apart at some secluded table of honor, but He got right in there with all those despised classes of society and treated them as His intimate friends, because He cared deeply about them. The way Jesus behaved at the feast, the way Jesus related to his friends, provided a source of constant inspiration to Matthew from that time forward. And Matthew went on to become one of Christ's most devoted evangelists.

But Matthew wanted to do one more thing to show his appreciation to Jesus for calling him to discipleship. He wanted to let the whole world know what kind of person Jesus was and the beautiful things Jesus said. So Matthew decided to write a book about Jesus, and because of that we have the Gospel of Matthew. Matthew records more of Jesus' sayings than any other gospel writer. We might have missed much had it not been for the fact that one day long ago Jesus looked beyond a man's despised employment and saw the man. He saw Matthew's tremendous potential, and despite personal risk, Jesus said, "I love you," even though it was a most socially questionable thing to do.

Chapter 8

One Way to Stop a Procession

The family line had ended. He, her only son, was dead. It had been bad enough at her husband's death, but she still had the boy then. But now he too was gone, and she was all alone. She walked ahead of the coffin. All Jewish women had to head the funeral processions, since supposedly they were the ones who brought sin into the world. The mother shuddered to think that she could possibly be the cause of such a death. It was far too bitter a role to play. Only a few days before he had been the epitome of health and vigor, a youth about to reach his prime. She had been so proud of him. The future had looked bright.

But then the fever had struck, and he had slipped from her. It had caused her great agony to watch him go. Even now she could hardly believe God would allow such a calamity to fall. And what would she do to make a living?

Women during the first century had a hard time finding employment. Would she have to survive on the mercy of others? But those fears were nothing compared with the aching void she felt within. He was gone!

Her eyes blinded with tears, she stumbled on. "He's gone. He's gone! He's *gone!*" pounded in her numb mind. Oblivious to the people around her, she only knew she must put one foot in front of the other one—she had to make it to the place of burial. The melancholy tinkle of cymbals and the mournful melody of the flutes added to her grief, and she could hardly bear to listen to the frenzied, shrill cries of the professional mourners. Their grief seemed so artificial, almost a sacrilege. How could they possibly know the pain, the horrible loss of a widow's only son?

And then He stood beside her. In one of the kindest voices she had ever heard in her entire life, He whispered tenderly, "Don't cry." From anyone else those words would have been sheer mockery, but something about His voice made her stop and listen. The words carried such feeling. She blinked away her tears as best she could in order to see who had spoken to her. And then she heard the crowd gasp.

Quickly she turned, just in time to see Jesus touch the wicker coffin. What could this man mean? The crowd looked shocked. The audacity, the blasphemy, to stop a funeral procession. They could hardly believe their eyes. Touching a dead body represented the worst form of ceremonial defilement, requiring seven days of ceremonial purification before the person could return to society. But where it involved human need, Jesus didn't care about ceremonial uncleanness. The woman's plight deeply moved Him—He *had* to do something to help her. The crowd waited expectantly.

Jesus bent gently over the coffin. "Young man, get up!" The crowd held their breath. The boy stirred, then sat up and began talking. Everyone gasped. Were they seeing things? Was it mass hypnosis? Awestruck, they began praising God. "A great prophet has arisen among us and God has turned His face toward His people." But the mother was more than awed—she was overjoyed. Her son was alive. Jesus smiled and gave the boy back to his mother.

No one had asked Him to perform the miracle. But as He viewed the pathos of the poor widow, compassion filled Him. With tender sympathy He changed her grief to joy, risking ceremonial defilement and the disapproval of the crowd. And with delight He presented her son.

Chapter 9

New Life for a Little Girl

The unorthodoxy of the "rebel" rabbi, Jesus, had caused concern and suspicion for Jairus, one of the synagogue presidents. The official in charge of public worship, he had to carefully screen the synagogue service. Most men of his respected class hated and despised Jesus. And Jairus had to admit that he himself hadn't responded too favorably to Him at times.

But none of that mattered now. At home his twelve-year-old daughter, his only child, lay all but dead, and Jairus was nearly frantic. Forgetting the fact that he was president of the board of elders and had all the pride and prejudice that went along with that job, Jairus threw himself at the feet of Jesus. "My little girl is dying," he cried. "Will You come and put Your hands on her—then she will get better and live." He didn't care what the people thought—he *had* to save his little girl.

And I love Jesus' response. He could have said, "Well, I see you're quite willing to use Me for emergency-room services, even though I'm a little too unorthodox to fit into the synagogue. If I'm unsafe in orthodox places, I'm too dangerous to help you too." But instead, He asked no questions, laid out no conditions. Jesus immediately went home with Jairus.

However, the crowds blocked the streets so that Jesus could hardly move. What agony Jairus must have gone through as he felt the precious moments slip away, knowing that in just a few more minutes his daughter would breathe her last breath unless Jesus could get to her. And finally the news came: "Your daughter is dead. There is no need to bother the master any further." It was too late. Heartbroken, Jairus started to slip away when Jesus caught him.

"Now don't be afraid, just go on believing." Jesus urged him to have faith, helped him to have faith, that all would be well. Finally they arrived at Jairus' home.

Despair infected it. The hired mourners and flutists had arrived and had already begun their mournful wailing. The simulated grief, the torn clothes, and the loud shrieking jarred Jesus' quiet soul. "Why are you making such a noise with your crying?" He queried. "The child is not dead; she is fast asleep." The mourners laughed. It was obvious the girl was dead.

Jesus requested them to leave. Their fake grief would interfere with what He planned to do. Instead He took only Jairus and his wife, plus Peter, James, and John (three witnesses were needed to verify a report) into the little girl's bedroom. Not fearing ritual defilement, Jesus bent down and took the little dead hand in His. Then in the familiar language of her home, probably using the same words her mother had used to awaken her every morning, Jesus whispered tenderly, "Time to get up, little one."

Suddenly she stirred. Then she jumped out of bed and started walking around the room. Everyone stared, speechless; her parents were nearly overcome with joy. But now that He had brought her back to life, Jesus was thoughtful to see that she regained her strength. With tender regard for the practical, He ordered the family to give her something to eat. It would also give her mother something tangible to do to help calm her excitement. Then with one final touch of sensitivity He suggested that they should not let anyone know what had happened, for she didn't need a lot of publicity. He wanted the little girl to live a normal life, not as some circus freak, the object of everyone's curiosity, but as a regular Jewish girl facing the dawn of womanhood.

Chapter 10

The End of Doctor Bills

"I must get through to Him," she told herself, and she drove herself a little harder despite her exhaustion. "If only I can touch His clothes," she kept saying, "I shall be all right." It was her only hope. For twelve years she had wandered from doctor to doctor trying to find a cure. Even though she had spent her entire life savings on medical bills, she was not any better. On the contrary, she was getting worse. She felt tremendously discouraged about it all.

But her hopes had revived again when she heard of the miracles Christ performed. Perhaps if He could cleanse a leper, He could free her from her disease too, even though she suffered from a woman's problem. She had had her menstrual period continuously for twelve years. Such hemorrhaging made her life a burden. Most women suffered one week out of every month—but twelve years?

In a continual state of anemia, she was quite weak. But besides the physical discomfort of her problem, it had virtually made her an outcast from society, for she was continuously ceremonially unclean. Anything she touched became unclean, and anyone who touched her until she was free from her malady was defiled. No one associated with her anymore. Unable even to share her feelings of discouragement with friends, she might as well have been a leper.

Christ was her only hope. She felt sure that if she could only get to Him, He could heal her. When He had taught by the sea, she had tried to get through the crowds to Him, but it had been too much for her in her weakened physical condition. Now as He left the house of Levi-Matthew, she tried again to press through the crowd, but it was hopeless. She was about ready to give up in despair. Suddenly He passed almost beside her, but she couldn't speak. How could she explain her problem in front of all those strangers? And how would He react to her telling Him about such a problem? It was too risky and embarrassing. "If only I can touch His clothes, I shall be all right," she told herself.

Summoning all her strength she leaned forward. In one final frantic stretch she managed to touch just the hem of His coat. But that touch concentrated the faith of a lifetime. Immediately she felt a flash of electric force pass through her system, and she was healed. Her pain and her feeling of physical exhaustion vanished. She was a new person. In silent gratitude, she began to withdraw from the crowd.

But suddenly Jesus stopped. He turned around, His eyes searching the multitude. "Who touched Me?" He said in a clear voice. She trembled. The crowds stared in amazement at Jesus, and Peter put their incredulity into words. "Master, remember that You're in a crowd. There're people all around You, jostling You from every side . . . "

"But someone touched Me, for I felt power going out from Me," Jesus replied.

The woman knew she must acknowledge that she was the one who had touched Him. Approaching Him, she fell at His feet, scared to death. In faltering speech she told Him the whole story. She shook uncontrollably, waiting for Him to denounce her for making Him ritually unclean, for her touch of faith had been enough to contaminate Him according to the Jewish ceremonial law. In terror she waited for Him to vent His anger.

But Jesus, determined that her faith should not go unnoticed, said tenderly to her, "Daughter, it is your faith that has healed you. Go home in peace, and be free from your trouble." She could hardly believe her ears. He had called her *daughter*—had personally recognized her, an outcast of society for twelve years, as His daughter. Jesus had praised her for her faith. His words brought comfort and lasting joy. She would never forget this day.

Chapter 11

It's OK—Take a Break

They had just returned from the tour. In a way it was more like field-school evangelism. But that doesn't matter much. The disciples were back home, and they had some pretty exciting stories to tell.

I can imagine that they were literally bursting inside, eager to share their experiences with their best friend, Jesus. James and John, typical "sons of thunder" that they were, had probably had a number of successful meetings where they had thundered out the Good News. Perhaps Judas, since he was treasurer for the group, had been more involved in the Ingathering-type thing, collecting money for the poor. And Thomas, good old doubting Thomas, had felt skeptical of the entire enterprise. Whatever their experiences had been, the disciples were glad to be back again in the security of Jesus' presence.

They were worn out, too. It had been difficult to get along with nothing but a staff—no bread, no bag, no money in their belts, not even a change of clothes. To have people deride them was hard to bear. And being with people and trying to meet all their many needs had taken a lot out of them. The disciples were physically, mentally, and emotionally drained.

Immediately sensitive to their needs, Jesus saw that they needed a break. He knew how exhausted they were, but He also realized they wouldn't get any rest if they stayed with Him in that place. Extremely busy Himself, He scarcely had time to eat. Life was hectic around Jesus. Dozens of people waited for healing. Lepers wailed, "Unclean," in the distance. Pharisees hovered around like hawks, ready to pounce at His slightest error, arguing, muttering under their breaths. Jesus did not want to subject His tired disciples to all that hassle; so He said to them, "Come away by yourselves to a lonely place, and rest a while."

Together they climbed into a boat and crossed the Lake of Galilee to a lovely quiet little spot near Bethsaida. It was spring, and the countryside was alive and beautiful, a refreshing sight to the weary disciples. To this secluded place they had come to get away from it all, to rest, to rejuvenate their souls, to learn from their mistakes, and to catch a brighter vision. Here they could be together, alone. Alone with Jesus. He had much to share with them. And He wanted them to know that it was OK to take a break once in a while, that it was proper to recharge one's batteries periodically. Better than anyone else, He knew what it was like to be totally drained, and He cared enough about His disciples to give them some time to unwind.

Chapter 12

Soothing Hunger Pains

They'd been standing all day in the hot sun—mobs of them—probably ten thousand in all. But they hadn't really noticed that until now. The pictures of the kingdom of God that the Great Teacher had been describing to them all day had kept their thoughts occupied. The stories of the buried treasure, the sower, the pearl of great price, had fascinated them so much that they had forgotten the time of day and the fact that they were famished.

Jesus realized that they were hungry. He might have viewed them with disdain. After all, He Himself was a superfaster—He'd gone for forty days without as much as a morsel of food. The people couldn't take anything—not even one day of starvation. But instead, He watched them—weary and faint, or as the Bible says, "like sheep without a shepherd"—and felt concern about their physical needs. To Him, merely feeding them spiritual truths was not enough. He *cared* about the fact that they were hungry.

And so He said to Philip, "Where can we buy food for these people to eat?" After all, Philip was the logical one to ask. Since he was a native of the area, he'd be well acquainted with all the bakeries in town. Philip glanced at Him in amazement. Perhaps the hot sun had gotten to Jesus, or was it that He too suffered from low-blood sugar? It was absolutely absurd to think of finding that much bread in Bethsaida after walking the distance before nightfall, and then trying to pay for it was another thing. The cost alone would be ridiculous. To feed ten thousand people even the simplest fare would have taken about a six-and-a-half-month salary.

"Are You feeling all right, Jesus?"

Then Andrew quietly said (and I'm sure he must have been embarrassed because it sounded so ridiculous), "Lord, uh, there's a boy here who has five small barley loaves and a couple of pickled fish."

I can imagine the other disciples bursting out laughing. "Man, thanks a lot, Andrew—that's a mighty big help—five whole loaves, eh? and two pickled fish? Wow!"

But Jesus said, "Get the people to sit down." And here's another thing I like about Jesus—He was so organized. He had the disciples arrange the people in groups of fifty to serve them more efficiently. Everybody sat down. Jesus took the loaves, gave thanks for them, and started distributing them to the disciples, and He distributed the fish in the same way. For a couple of hours that day He turned the disciples into waiters. They fed ten thousand people in record time.

And the neat thing about it all was that Jesus didn't

merely sustain the people, but He *filled* them. Jesus could have told them, "Now just a crust for everyone—let's not be greedy—let's all just take enough to tide us over until we get home." But Jesus didn't say that. True, the menu was humble. Barley bread was the staple food of the poor, who usually ate it with pickled fish as a sort of relish. No, the meal wasn't exactly caviar, but it was food and plenty of it. So much, in fact, that the disciples filled twelve baskets with pieces left over. Everyone was satisfied.

But then a beautiful thing happened. The people, deeply moved by Jesus' miracle of love, wanted to share what He had taught them. Excitedly they approached Him. "Jesus, there are some poor hungry people in our home villages. Do You think we could take some of the leftover food to them?" Overjoyed by their response, Jesus again distributed His food among the people. Perhaps His real miracle that day was to fill the people's hearts with so much love that suddenly they wanted to reach out with the touch of love to their fellowmen.

Chapter 13

The Water-Walker

It was almost five miles across the Sea of Galilee to Capernaum. Normally they could easily cover the distance in an hour. But not this time. They had rowed for almost eight hours now and were about ready to give up. Even experienced fishermen like Peter, Andrew, James, and John had used up all their skill. At the mercy of the lake now, they knew they couldn't keep the craft together much longer. How they wished Jesus were with them!

And suddenly He was there. They didn't recognize Him at first, for He came in rather a strange way. Jesus, with His typical creativity, had chosen to walk on the water. And you'll have to admit that at three o'clock in the morning after you've battled boisterous waves for your lives, seeing a figure in a white robe walking calmly on waves that have almost been your undoing would be a bit unsettling. The terrified disciples screamed, "It's a ghost!"

But immediately Jesus tenderly calmed their fears. "It's OK," He said. "It's just I. Don't be afraid."

And Peter, recognizing his Lord, was almost overcome with joy. So overwhelmed was he, in fact, that he did something a little ridiculous. He cried out, "Lord, if it's really You, . . . tell me to come to You on the water."

"Come," replied Jesus.

So Peter stepped out of the boat. For a little while Peter was quite a water-walker. He just kept looking at Jesus and taking steps.

But all of a sudden the thought crossed his mind, "Hmmm, not bad for a first try. Say, I'm quite good at this. I wonder if the gang in the boat has noticed my new ability." He turned around to see if the others in the boat *had* noticed. But instead of them, he saw the waves whipping viciously around him. Suddenly he realized where he was—right in the middle of the lake *on foot* (enough to make anybody sink). He forgot all about Jesus and started worrying, then whoosh! down he went.

But the instant Peter started sinking, he cried out, "Lord, save me!" and Jesus did. In fact, the Bible says Jesus *immediately* stretched forth His hand and caught Peter.

Now if it had been left up to me, I probably would have let Peter gurgle just a little—you know, to teach him a good lesson. Or I might have said, "Sorry, brother. If you're stupid enough to walk on the water and forget about me, then you can just save yourself."

But Jesus didn't let Peter go under or even lecture him. Instead He gave him the help he needed.

Chapter 14

Even Some Dog Food

Jesus was tired. It seemed as though He and His disciples had worked night and day recently. So they decided to get away to the neighborhood of Tyre, a remote place where they might have a chance to get some rest. Christ even requested that they keep their whereabouts secret. But it wasn't long before a woman followed them, crying at the top of her lungs, "Lord, son of David, have pity on me! My daughter is in a terrible state—a devil has got into her!" Someone, and a strange foreign woman at that, had interrupted Jesus again.

At first Jesus seemed totally to ignore her. He acted as if He hadn't even heard her request. But His silence seemed only to challenge her more. She persisted in pleading for His help. Finally the disciples, tired of her pathetic cry, begged Jesus, "Do send her away—she's still following us and calling out."

With mock harshness, Jesus said to her, "I was only sent to the lost sheep of the house of Israel." Ordinarily such a comment, accompanied by His previous silence, would have been enough to put anyone off. However, the mere fact that He, a Jew, would even stop to dialogue with her, a Syrophoenician, one of the hated ancestral enemies of the Jews, gave her much encouragement. In His face "she saw a compassion that He could not hide" (*The Desire of Ages*, p. 401). Something in the tone of His voice, the look in His eye, made her keep on pleading with utter eloquence, "Lord, help me."

Jesus continued by quoting this old Jewish proverb: "It's not right, you know, . . . to take the children's food and throw it to the dogs." It was a deadly insult—or it could have been—for dogs in those days were lean, savage scavengers of the streets. But with whimsical tenderness, Jesus switched the word for dogs so that instead of using the one for dogs of the street, He employed the word that referred to little pet dogs. The word-switch had the effect of taking the harshness, the pain out of the proverb, reducing it to basically say, "Children shouldn't feed pet doggies at the table."

In witty response, she willingly accepted the "doggie" label, and matched proverb with proverb. "Yes, Lord, I know, but even the dogs live on the scraps that fall from their master's table!"

Her response absolutely delighted Jesus. Pleased with her perseverance and her faith, fascinated by her quickness of wit, He liked the way she wouldn't take no for an answer. Refusing to make her wait a moment longer, He eagerly told her, "If you can answer like that, you can go home. The evil spirit has left your daughter." He appreciated her humor, and the way she played along with Him helped Him show His disciples the difference between the typical Jewish attitude toward a Gentile and His own. Jesus rewarded her amply, even though she had merely asked for crumbs. When she arrived home, her daughter was resting quietly, free from the evil spirit that had previously haunted her soul.

Christ had tested the Canaanite woman differently from most people. He had used playful wit and sarcasm to reach her. Yet underneath the humor His gentle sensitivity had come through as usual. And although she was a woman, a Gentile, who had insisted on interrupting His rest, He was as willing to help her as He was anyone else. She needed Him, and that was all that mattered.

Chapter 15

Silenced by Shorthand in the Sand

She was stunned. Only minutes before she had lain in a passionate embrace—a quiet, secret moment. Then suddenly she heard crashing and shouting, and the next thing she knew, it seemed the entire Sanhedrin had burst into her bedroom. They had caught her in the act. And now they dragged her, half naked, through the crowded streets, their eager fingers digging into her flesh. Not only was she still in shock from her rude awakening, but she was also well aware of the penalty for women caught in adultery. Death—death by stones. But where? How? Why? Question after question flashed through her mind. She felt a thousand eyes upon her, and she struggled desperately to get away from the men. But her struggles only made them grasp her with greater ferocity. Their laughter rang harsh and cruel.

Suddenly she realized that they had trapped her—that

she was a victim of another of their plots to trip up Jesus of Nazareth. For here they were, in Temple Square, the most public square in all the city, standing before Him and asking for His judgment concerning her sins. She knew it was no use to plead for mercy—she was only a woman. Falling to the ground in front of Jesus, trembling with fright, she waited for Him to curse her and let fly with the first stone.

But then the woman looked into His face, and she knew she would never be the same again. She had expected to see a harsh, stern face of justice, with flashing cruel eyes. But instead she saw a face filled with compassion, with tender concern. His kind eyes spoke more of mercy than of justice. With one look at that beautiful face, the woman saw herself for the sinner she was. Knowing she deserved no mercy, she waited for His sentence.

Meanwhile the men pressed Jesus for His verdict. "What do *You* think, sir?" The woman listened for His answer. "Please, sir, what *is* Your ruling in this matter?" The crowds pressed closer.

Jesus said, "Let him who is without sin cast the first stone at her." She cringed in anticipation of the deathblow. But no stones fell.

Then came gasps of surprise, almost of horror, and she heard their robes swishing and the sounds of departing footsteps. Turning she saw in the sand where Jesus had casually been writing little hints about the guilty secrets of the men's lives.

The next thing she knew He bent over her. "Doesn't anyone accuse you?" He whispered softly.

Looking up again at Him, she quavered, "No one,

sir." But that was not enough—and with sobbing, she poured out the ugly secrets of her life. She declared herself a sinner. It had taken only a look at Christ for her to see herself as she really was.

With eyes filled with love, He looked straight into her face and said, "I know you're all of those things. But I don't condemn you, for I have bigger dreams for you in My kingdom. Just don't get involved like that again." At last, in His eyes, she saw what she might become through Him. It was a vision she would never forget.

Chapter 16

Always Time for Children

The disciples glared at the crowd of women and children waiting to see Jesus. Jesus was far too busy to cater to the trivial requests of a bunch of women and kids. After all, it was really the disciples' duty to screen the innumerable problems that people came to Jesus with. They were only trying to protect Him, to cut down His work load a little. A totally unnecessary interruption, the mothers and children were such a nuisance. Impatiently the disciples began shooing them away. "Go on, now. Jesus simply doesn't have time for you. Hurry along."

The mothers turned away, disappointed. Several of the children began to cry—they had wanted so much to see their Jesus again. It was a custom for parents to have the children blessed by a rabbi, and these mothers had wanted theirs blessed by Jesus. He had made a great difference in their lives, in their communities. During the past couple years they had watched all the beautiful things He had done. He had cleansed a leper, raised the dead, healed diseases, given a comforting touch to many a sad soul. How special, they thought, to have their children blessed by His beautiful hands! But it was not to be—He was too busy.

Suddenly they heard His voice. It was indignant. Turning around, they saw Him talking to the disciples. "You must let little children come to Me—*never* stop them!" He insisted. He seemed angry to think that anyone should consider children unimportant. His disciples had completely misunderstood His priorities. To Him, no one, especially children, was insignificant or a nuisance. One little boy sensing Jesus' welcome earlier than the others, hurried to His side. Smilingly, Jesus stooped to pick him up, and turning once again to the disciples, said quietly, "Never forget, the kingdom of heaven is like this."

With delight the mothers saw the disciples beckoning them to return. The children started running. Jesus opened His arms, and in moments children surrounded Him. The kindness in His face, His gentleness, His willingness to take time to listen to their questions, had won their confidence. They knew He loved them. One by one He picked each one up and held him close, tenderly placing His hands on each head, softly whispering words of individual blessing, sharing His dreams with each one. He loved to cuddle them close to His heart. To each mother, too, He offered tender words of encouragement, eased her worries, comforted her in her concerns. With exquisite sensitivity He let them know that He understood what they were going through and that He cared and was willing to help.

Patiently He answered the children's countless questions. In fact, He seemed eagerly to await them. Continually He sought to simplify what He was saying so that the children, too, could understand the big ideas He had in mind. He willingly brought His teachings down to their level. It was important to Him for the children to know that what He came to give, they were not too young to receive.

Willingly He listened to what they had to say, accepted the flowers they brought to Him, and even found time to play with them. They loved Him dearly. And many would remember the day He held them tightly in His arms and whispered those special words of blessing, those special dreams.

This scene is especially significant to me when I realize that Jesus was on His way to Jerusalem to die. To think that Jesus, at a time of tension and agony, had time for children is a beautiful thought indeed. How special that one of the last acts of His life was to hold children in His arms.

Chapter 17

Too Big a Decision

Many times he had stood at the edge of the crowd listening to what the Master had to say. Everything He said struck an answering chord in the heart of the rich young ruler. Deep inside, the young man longed to be one of Jesus' disciples. He had a noble personality, and the community highly respected him. It was rare that one so young should have such a position of responsibility as a member of the honored council of the Jews, but he had conscientiously lived an exemplary life, worthy of his excellent reputation. As he watched the last of the children go away after the beautiful scene of Jesus' love to them, the rich young man could hold back no longer. In a burst of impulse he dashed through the crowd with youthful eagerness and fell at Jesus' feet. It was quite a sight to see the well-dressed aristocrat in the prime and strength of his youth kneeling at the feet of the poor, unlicensed Jesus.

But Jesus was excited. Here was no leper, blind man, cripple, or notorious tax collector. Jesus had great dreams for him.

The young ruler began with a burst of rather manipulative flattery. "Good Master, tell me, please, what must I do to be sure of eternal life?" It was unheard of to address a Jewish rabbi that way. *Good* was an adjective reserved for God. But Jesus would not fall for such devices.

Instead, He forced the ruler to back up and consider the implications of what he had just said. "No flattery, please. Don't call Me *good.* Save that word for God unless you're willing to accept Me as God. I cannot help you if you consider Me to be merely a teacher." It troubled Him that the young leader assumed he could earn eternal life.

But Jesus, willing to touch the young man on his level, answered his question in terms of doing. "If you want to enter that life you must keep the commandments." Then Jesus carefully chose the commandments that involve man's duty to man. "Do no murder, Do not commit adultery, Do not steal, Do not bear false witness, Do not cheat, Honor your father and mother"—the commandments that dealt with personal relationships with others, because Jesus had already sensed where the young man's problem lay. He longed for him to recognize his deficiency. Thus with tender subtleness He presented those things which might touch the young man's vulnerable spot.

But the young man, somewhat impatient with the simplicity of Jesus' reply, pressed further. "I have carefully kept all these," he said. "What is still missing in my life?"

Jesus looked at him with extreme earnestness. In him He saw just the sort of man He needed in His ministry. So much potential for good dwelt there. Jesus' heart went out to him in a special way. With direct conciseness He gave the young ruler a short, crucial test of his true condition. "There is one thing you still need. Go and sell everything you have, give the money away to the poor—you will have riches in heaven. And then come back and follow Me." Eagerly Jesus wanted to show him that respectability is not sufficient, that it is not enough to obey the letter of the law, to avoid hurting and hating his fellowman. He sought to show him that goodness is active, that the real test is how much good one has done for people. It was an appeal of love, a plea for the young man to put people ahead of things.

A pained look came across the young ruler's face. He had expected some grandiose mission bordering on the heroical, not something as painful as giving up those things so dear to him, those things he had worked so hard to acquire. Intense sadness haunted his eyes—it was too high a price to pay. Jesus had touched a sensitive nerve. It was painful for the young man to realize that he couldn't keep his wealth and serve God fully at the same time. Crestfallen, he bowed his head and quietly walked away, a different person from the eager young man who had burst on the scene moments earlier.

With intense agony Jesus watched him go. How much He wanted that young man as part of His inner circle! He had so much potential, and Jesus loved him greatly. It must have been hard for Jesus not to go after him, to work out a compromise. But Jesus never coerced anyone, even though people's choices often hurt Him deeply. While it was difficult for Him to see them deliberately choose to fail to be all that they could be, yet He jealously guarded their freedom of choice. Although Jesus would do anything to make the alternatives clearer, the final decision rested with the individual. Although He might want something for a person very badly, He never forced anything on another.

Chapter 18

Invitation to Dinner Reversed

Zacchaeus stood on his tiptoes, straining to catch a glimpse of the Great Teacher, but it was no use—he was just too short. By now he'd gotten used to the fact that he was the runt in the crowd, the man who came up to other men's armpits. But today it was different—he *had* to see. Frenziedly he had tried to press through the crowd, but Passover pilgrims and the regular riffraff of the city jammed the narrow streets of Jericho. Besides, no one would think of letting the "clever little crook" through. After the way he'd ripped them off in his tax-collecting business, why should they do him a favor?

They hated him. A heathen dog, that's what he was. Not only was he a publican, but he was the head publican, who ran a big enough business to have men working under him. Jericho, being the port of entry for all traffic crossing the Jordan River from the east side, was an ideal place for a tax collector and customs officer to make money, and Zacchaeus had taken full advantage of the situation. In fact, he was one of the richest men in town, which made them despise him all the more. People considered him a traitor to his nation, as they did all publicans. His name was a joke around town. *Zacchaeus*—it meant "pure." "A *pure* thief is right!" several had commented. Few names could have been more unsuitable.

But that didn't change things now. He had to see Jesus. The words of John the Baptist in the wilderness had touched Zacchaeus. John had advised him and his fellow publicans, "You must not demand more than you are entitled to." And Zacchaeus had really attempted to play it straight from that point onward. In fact, he even had tried to make amends for some of his past cheating. But no one would trust him. No one could believe that he was trying to make things right. As far as they were concerned, once a publican always a publican. Whoever heard of a publican repenting? Any publican who put on a repentance show was simply playing another game to trick the people out of their money. Zacchaeus trying to make things right? Incredible! What a laugh!

But ever since John the Baptist's preaching, Zacchaeus *had* struggled to make things right. It was discouraging, though, constantly to encounter suspicion and distrust when he sought to do the right thing. At times it was enough to make anyone give up and simply go back to living the kind of life people expected of him. Zacchaeus had begun to wonder if any hope existed for him, if it was possible for him, a publican, to truly reform. Had God, like the Jewish leaders, forsaken him?

That's why he had to see Jesus, for in Him lay his last bit of hope. One of Jesus' most trusted disciples was a publican. Could it be that he, Zacchaeus, chief of publicans, might also have a chance at repentance? Could Jesus transform his life, too? If only he could catch a glimpse of Jesus' face, he would know the answer.

But he was too short; all he could see were the people in front of him. It was a discouraging position. Suddenly an idea struck him. His eyes sparkled, and quickly he retreated from the crowd. Taking a back street, he ran several blocks ahead of the crowd to the old sycamore fig tree he had loved to climb when a child. He remembered how he used to sit in its branches for hours, watching the people go by on the main highway—it had been a good vantage point. And despite the fact that he was one of the best-dressed men in town, he began to shin up the tree. It must have seemed a ridiculous sight to see a middle-aged, well-dressed little man trying to climb a tree. But Zacchaeus didn't care what he looked like or what people thought of him. Besides, he had gone far enough ahead of the crowd so that few people saw him up there anyway.

The crowd came by, and Zacchaeus, catching his glimpse of Jesus, knew the answer to his question. It was almost too much for his heart to hold. But that wasn't the end. Just as Jesus passed directly under the old fig tree, He stopped. Zacchaeus held his breath, afraid to move a muscle for fear that Jesus would notice him. But it didn't help, for Jesus glanced upward. The eyes of the crowd followed the direction of His gaze, and the snickering began, for Zacchaeus, up a tree, did look a bit strange.

But Jesus didn't snicker. Instead, He looked directly into Zacchaeus' eyes and said, "Zacchaeus, hurry up and come down. I'm going to your place for dinner." Zacchaeus could hardly believe his ears. Jesus had called him by name. How did He know it? And not only that. Jesus wanted to go to his place for dinner. Going to someone's place for dinner represented one of the most intimate things friends could do—and Jesus was willing to do that with him, a despised publican! In fact, He had even invited Himself over.

Zacchaeus pinched himself to make sure he was experiencing reality. It was more than he had ever hoped for. He had hoped only for a glimpse of Jesus, and here he was getting Him for a houseguest. Suddenly the goodness of God overwhelmed him, and Zacchaeus cried out, "Look sir, I will give half my property to the poor. And if I have swindled anybody out of anything, I will pay him back four times as much." That was a generous offer. The law required only that a thief restore double the amount taken. But Zacchaeus, touched by Christ's accepting him as a close friend, wanted to show his gratitude.

The tax collector's response touched Jesus, and He did one more thing for the little man. He turned to the crowds, by then shocked beyond words that Jesus would willingly eat at the house of such a sinner, and He said, "Salvation has come to this house today! Zacchaeus is a descendant of Abraham." The publican could not have asked for a more beautiful affirmation. To a Jew, few things were more important than being a descendant of Abraham. However, although Zacchaeus was a Jew, the synagogue had excommunicated him because of his profession. They considered him cut off, a heathen dog, no longer worthy to be a descendant of Abraham. But now Jesus was telling him—and not only him but the whole crowd in

Jericho—that everyone should once again regard Zacchaeus as a member of the family. Those words held tremendous reassurance for Zacchaeus—the outcast of society had been welcomed home. It seemed too good to be true. The little tax collector knew the answer to his question—it was possible for a publican to reform. God had not forsaken him.

I wish I could have been at Zacchaeus' house for dinner that night. I can see Zacchaeus putting on a spread beyond our wildest imagination. And the conversation—wow! Never had things at Zacchaeus' house been so lively. It was a night to remember.

Jesus had been willing to risk His entire reputation to give Zacchaeus that kind of a night. It scandalized the scribes and the rabbis to think that Jesus would dare to eat with such a heathen dog. And they viewed Him with contempt ever after—how else could one view a publican-lover? But Jesus didn't care about what they thought of Him; He cared about Zacchaeus. He saw that Zacchaeus needed special reassurance of God's love, and so He was willing to go the second mile to prove it to him.

Chapter 19

Extravagant Love

Jesus and Lazarus were the honored guests at the big feast that Simon the Pharisee had thrown for all his friends. Jesus had healed Simon of the dreaded disease of leprosy, and Simon had staged the feast to express his appreciation. Jesus had less than one week to live. It was the Saturday night preceding the Crucifixion.

Martha busily served at the head table. But Mary stood in the background quietly straining to hear every word that Jesus said. Today she would show Him how much she loved Him. She had much to be grateful for. He had brought Lazarus home to them from death, had forgiven her sins, and had always listened to her. And often she herself had sat at His feet listening. Deep inside she had a foreboding that He would not be with them much longer. Now she wanted to do something for Him to demonstrate her love before it was too late. For a long time she had saved her money to buy Him an alabaster box of costly perfume. In her hands she held the light gray translucent bottle containing the fragrant nard. The tiny bottle and its expensive contents represented much personal sacrifice.

With an exquisite sense of abandon she broke open the bottle. It was as though the room contained no one else but Jesus and her. With the unself-consciousness of deep love she poured the entire contents of the bottle on His feet and head. She had taken the most precious thing she possessed and spent it *all* on Jesus—had given the best she had. Her gratitude spilled over into tears. Having not realized she would need a towel, with spontaneous resourcefulness she quickly let down her long, flowing hair and began wiping His feet with it. It was a risky thing to do because her culture considered it immoral and disgraceful for a woman to let her hair down in public. But she didn't care—she was conscious only of her love for Jesus and her need to express this adoration.

She hadn't meant to make a scene—had only wanted it to be a private thing between her and Jesus. Unfortunately she'd forgotten that nard is so fragrant the smell would permeate the entire room. But it wasn't long before everyone sniffed and glared in her direction. The cruel words of Judas, "Why on earth wasn't this perfume sold?" jarred Mary to her senses. "It's worth a year's wages, which she could have given to the poor." His words stung her.

Mary trembled, waiting for Martha to start scolding her for her foolish extravagance. She worried, too, that Jesus would condemn her excessive spending—maybe she should have given it to the needy, even though she had only wanted to show her love in some tangible way. But

Jesus jumped to her defense. "Let her alone. Why must you make her feel uncomfortable? She has done a beautiful thing for Me. You have the poor with you always, and you can do good to them whenever you like, but you will not always have Me. She has done all she could, for she has anointed My body in preparation for burial. I assure you that wherever the gospel is preached throughout the whole world this deed will be recounted, as her memorial to Me."

Joy thrilled through Mary's being—Jesus had understood and appreciated her gift. He had correctly interpreted the meaning of her action and even given it greater significance than she had dreamed. After praising the beauty of her extravagant love, with exquisite sensitivity He did a special thing—He granted her act the immortality of memory. His words overwhelmed Mary. It was too much to ask, far beyond her wildest dreams.

He could have been embarrassed, especially after she had let her hair down. It was a rather indelicate situation. How do you explain the fact that some woman is pouring a whole bottle of expensive perfume all over you and fondling your feet besides? But instead of resenting the public display, He wholeheartedly accepted her gift and spiritedly defended her actions. Jesus treated it for what it was, an act of inspired devotion.

Yet in spite of His defense of Mary, He did not lash out at Judas and expose his pretense. Jesus could have unmasked him beautifully. But He remained silent, giving the disciple another opportunity to change his mind about Jesus.

Simon the Pharisee, too, had passed silent judgment on Jesus' treatment of the situation. Seeing Jesus allow a questionable woman to treat Him so intimately convinced Simon that Jesus was not a prophet, since He didn't seem to know what kind of person He had on His hands. Instead of openly rebuking his unbelief, Jesus simply told him a pointed little story. Simon caught the veiled rebuke, intensely grateful that Jesus had been kind enough not to expose him in front of all his guests. The Pharisee saw his mistake through the exercise of Jesus' pitying love and determined to make amends.

Throughout the feast Jesus dealt with each individual sensitively. Mary's act of devotion warmed His heart, for it would be one of the last kind things Jesus would ever have done for Him. Her extravagant love had meant much, and He was eager to let the whole world hear Him say thank you.

Chapter 20

One Last Meal

Jesus determined to make Thursday night a special night for all of them. It would be the last time that all thirteen of them would be together. In just a few more hours He would stand trial for His life. He so much wanted to spend His final moments in close fellowship with those He loved. He had a lot to share with them. But as He looked into the disciples' eyes, He grew strangely quiet.

What He wanted to tell them was far too precious, too close to His heart, to waste on minds occupied with other things. His heart ached—they had been fighting again—the same old thing about who was going to be who in His cabinet. Hostility and resentment ran high. It hurt Him to see them divided because of such pettiness. He had wanted so much for them to be close to one another during His final hours.

The major problem at the moment was that the group

had no slave available to wash the dust off their feet, and none of the disciples were about to play slave. The pitcher and big copper basin stood ready, waiting for someone to break down and serve. Jesus watched. Had the three years they had spent with Him been a waste of time? Had they missed the point of His entire ministry? How could He show them what love was all about? And then He knew.

Slowly He got up from the table and took off His robe. He slipped a towel around His waist and poured water into the basin. Every eye watched Him—what on earth did He plan to do? When He knelt down and began to wash Judas' feet, it almost blew the disciples' minds. Washing feet was a job reserved only for foreign slaves. The Jews didn't even require students to do it for their rabbi. Yet here was their Rabbi washing their dirty feet for them. Suddenly their hearts filled with guilt and shame. The thought of His incredible love was almost more than they could handle.

But Jesus kept on washing—the feet of His betrayer first, as if trying to say, "Oh, Judas, I care so much. You are very important to Me. How can I let you do what you're planning?" With tender hands—hands that had cleansed the lepers, stilled the seas, raised the dead—Jesus bathed the dirty feet of one who prepared to lead Him to His death. The touch of His kind hands, the sadness in His eyes, was almost enough to make Judas change his mind and confess his plottings, but his pride wouldn't let him. Quietly, almost sadly, Jesus went around the circle, washing twenty-four sweaty, dusty feet, pausing for a few precious minutes with each disciple and silently pleading for a new spirit free of pride and jealousy for that person. Everyone had a lot of time for thinking as Jesus washed all twelve disciples' feet, and by the time He finished, their mood had changed completely. They were ready to listen to Him. Somehow their places in His cabinet didn't seem so important anymore.

Finishing, He put on His robe again and sat down at the table. He paused for a moment and then said, "Men, do you know what I've done for you? If I, your Teacher and Lord, have washed your feet, you must be ready to wash one another's feet. It doesn't make you any less of a person. Remember that just as I have washed the dust from your feet, so I have cleansed you of your sins. Wash each other's feet often to remind yourselves that I have forgiven you." He thus instituted a special ordinance to prepare them for the beauty of the symbols of the wine and the bread—an ordinance that would help men remember to be good to one another because He had been good to them.

Finally they began to eat their Passover supper. It was a simple meal: roasted lamb, unleavened bread, bitter herbs, and grape juice. Jesus took a loaf of unleavened bread, offered a short blessing over it, and started to break it up. Giving a piece to each disciple, He said, "Take, eat; this is My body." Then He picked up the cup of grape juice, blessed it, and passed it around, saying, "Drink all of it, for this is My blood. I promise you I won't drink any more grape juice until we all drink it together in heaven. Every time you eat bread and drink grape juice, I want you to remember Me and the things we've shared together. Make it a special time."

Jesus wanted the disciples to remember the last meal they had together so that it would give them hope when the future looked dim. Every time they ate bread or drank grape juice, it would remind them of the date they had with Jesus to share those things together in heaven, of the love He had for them that Thursday night, and of the sacrifice He made for them because of that love.

Chapter 21

Agony in the Garden

They made their way to the Garden. It was a familiar path—they'd visited here many times before with Jesus, since it was one of His favorite spots. But tonight it was different—Jesus was strangely quiet. Something terrible bothered Him. They'd never seen Him like that before. A couple times they even had to catch Him or He would have fainted. He could hardly walk. Naturally, they felt concerned about Him.

As they came to the Garden gate, Jesus left eight of His disciples to pray there and then took Peter, James, and John into Gethsemane with Him. With painful honesty, He told them how He felt. "My heart is nearly breaking. Please stay here—you don't have to do anything except pray—just *be* with Me." He needed to feel that they were near to Him as He went through the agony of decision.

Because He couldn't bear to make His friends go

through the pain of what He had to face, He went about a stone's throw away and fell on the ground. It was horrible. Everything was at stake. The pressure He struggled under was unbelievable. Jesus seemed to be bearing every sin in the world, and the burden seemed to separate Him completely from His beloved Father. It felt like more than He could bear. Besides, He didn't want to die—He was still young. He still had much to do. And no one looked forward to death on the cross—the most dreaded form of death in the Eastern world. In His agony, Jesus dug His fingernails into the dirt as if to hang on to His life, His Father, just a little longer. Then from pale and trembling lips He gave an anguished cry: "Father, isn't there some way I can get out of this? I don't think I can go through with it—but if I must, Father, it's all right."

He needed to know that the people close to Him cared, to have assurance that they prayed for Him and themselves. With tremendous effort He staggered to His feet and stumbled painfully back to where He had left Peter, James, and John, longing to know that they were sympathizing with Him. But there they sprawled—out on the ground and snoring. Gently He awakened them. "Please stay awake with Me. I need you. You need to pray to make it." And then, instead of being bitter and wallowing in self-pity, muttering, "Nobody cares; nobody loves Me. They can't even stay awake for Me," He said, "I know that you meant to. It's just that you're so tired. Your spirit is willing, but human nature is weak." Even though He needed them greatly, He was willing to excuse their humanness, their lack of sympathy.

Again He returned to His place of struggle for an even greater battle. In fact, the tension, the agony of feeling separated from God, became so great that He literally began to sweat drops of blood. As heavy dew formed on the trees and dripped down upon Him, it seemed as if even nature cried in sympathy with Him. Once more He pleaded with God for a way out. Then, seeking comfort from His disciples, He sought them once more. They were sleeping. As they awakened they hardly recognized Him because of the changes in His face from the intense anguish He endured that night before His death. Ashamed by their weakness, they were speechless.

Jesus went back to His spot one more time, throwing Himself on the ground once again, fighting with Himself the most difficult battle of all. Everything appeared dark. He almost decided not to go through with His sacrifice. But as He saw the future, realized the helplessness of His children and how they would die without Him, He determined to go through with the plan of salvation. He would die so that we might live. After making His decision, He fainted.

God then did a special thing. He sent the angel Gabriel down to reassure Jesus of the closeness of the Father's love and to give Him the strength He needed to endure all that He would face in the next few hours. The comfort of the angel removed Jesus' depression and discouragement, and He was ready to defend His friends—ready to face His betrayer, Judas.

Chapter 22

The Call of Calvary

A crowd wound its way slowly through the streets of Jerusalem toward Golgotha—the Place of the Skull. Jesus headed for one of the most dreaded deaths in the ancient world. Moments before, the authorities had passed the fateful sentence, "You shall go to the cross." A soldier walked in front with a placard "describing" the crime. It said, "King of the Jews." They lay the cross roughly across Jesus' shoulders, but the events of the previous hours had taken their toll, and as soon as He felt its weight He fainted. The intense emotions, the long exhausting and brutal trials, the mental agony, the sleepless night, the pain and loss of blood from the scourgings, and the continual, cruel derision had so weakened Jesus that He could not carry it. The soldiers had to drag someone from the crowd to bear it the rest of the way.

As Jesus fainted under the burden of the cross, many

of the women in the crowd began to cry rather vocally. Despite the fact that He was almost delirious with pain and exhaustion and that He felt the overwhelming weight of the sins of the world upon His heart, their cries caught His attention. Jesus' ears were tuned to hear the faintest cry for help. As He listened to them sob He tenderly looked into their eyes. He knew that the wrong reasons motivated their pity, but that didn't matter. It made Him want to reach out a little farther to touch them in sympathy. "Women of Jerusalem, don't cry for Me. Cry for you and for your children." He proceeded, in love, to warn them of the coming destruction of Jerusalem.

After taking the "criminals" by the longest possible route to Golgotha, as was the custom of execution processions, they finally arrived at the site. The guards nailed Jesus, and bound the two thieves to their crosses. With painful precision the Roman soldier pounded a spike through each quivering hand. Then they spiked His feet to the wood. In one moment of supreme anguish, He felt the cross elevated and plunged with brutal unconcern into its hole. Yet through it all, Jesus remained quiet. As the soldiers hoisted His cross into position in the middle of the thieves, signifying Him to be the rankest criminal of the group, and dropped it into place He whispered a gasping prayer, "Father, forgive them; they do not know what they are doing."

The vigil began. Just a few feet below, the priests and rulers and the rabble hissed out their obscenities, scoffing, badgering, mocking. The hell of the cross had just begun. His arms and shoulder muscles bore the full brunt of the weight of His body. He hung there, suspended in midair, unable to move or change positions, cramped forever.

The weight of His body tore the flesh around the nails in His hands. The sun was fearfully hot, but as the blood and perspiration poured down His face and forehead, He had no free hands to wipe His face. The flies crawled mercilessly across His face and body, and again He was helpless to shoo them away. A blazing, raging thirst obsessed Him in the heat. The weight of His body on His diaphragm made every breath a gasping effort. Blood gorged the veins and arteries at His feet. He grew dizzy from loss of blood, the heat of the sun, and the intense agony of His ordeal. Meanwhile the crowd continued to taunt Him brutally. Yet through it all His thoughts were, "Father, forgive them; they do not know what they are doing."

One of the thieves heard His prayer. The words struck his heart like an arrow, forcing him to turn to this Man who could love so much. Immediately he saw the evil of his own life. In those final moments of his life he longed to be a different person. With intense anguish he cried out in hopeful desperation, "Jesus, remember me when You come into Your kingdom."

Jesus responded instantly. In a voice filled with compassion, He whispered, "I tell you truly today; you will be with Me in Paradise." He didn't worry about the thief's sordid past, nor was He concerned about the fact that just a few minutes earlier the thief had derided Him like all the rest. Rather, He accepted the thief's confession as sincere and immediately gave him the reassurance he needed.

Time passed, and the torture of the cross grew worse. Every breath was painful, each hand tore a little more, and a pool of blood formed at the foot of the cross. His thirst was unbearable. Jesus' eyes focused and refocused.

Seeing His mother standing there with John, the disciple He loved most, He tried to speak, but every word spelled intense agony. She also suffered as though she too were being crucified. But she could do nothing to ease His pain—could only silently wait there, watching His life slip from her. In deep sympathy He felt her pain, the torment of her soul. With supreme effort He gasped out His love to her. Nodding His head in John's direction, He said, "Mother, there is your son." And to John, He said, "And there is your mother." In His hour of deepest pain and anguish He remembered His mother, ensuring her that she would receive loving care for the rest of her life. He did not leave her homeless, but gave her a son to take His place. And to John He left a living memorial of His love—His mother. Together they would share their loneliness and be comforted.

Darkness fell thickly about the cross. A few more hours passed. Then came a violent earthquake—as though all nature reacted in sympathy with Jesus' sufferings. Jesus felt that sin had eternally separated Him from His Father, and the mental torture of that thought was so great that He hardly felt the physical pain any more. But He had done all He could. Man's salvation was sure. His final thoughts amid the horrible anguish of Crucifixion had been to forgive, to bless, to care for others.

Chapter 23

The Morning After

Imagine how the disciples and the women felt that Friday night. I doubt that anyone slept much. Even though Jesus had warned them about His death, they hadn't believed Him. They had other plans for Him. He was supposed to be their hero who would save them from the terrible Romans.

All through the Crucifixion they kept expecting Him to save Himself. But at three o'clock that afternoon He let out an anguished cry, "It is finished," and His head had dropped to His chest. He was dead. They knew everything had been poised to kill Him—the tremendous emotional burden, the ordeal of scourging, the loss of blood from the nails, dehydration, the exposure to the elements—it was enough to kill any man, but they hadn't expected Jesus to succumb. It surprised even Pilate that Jesus could die in six hours. Most criminals lived on for two or three days. But the fact was, Jesus was dead! And all His friends' hopes and dreams died with Him.

It had been a rush job to get Him buried before Sabbath. The disciples felt intense gratitude for the help of Nicodemus and Joseph of Arimathea. Joseph had provided a tomb, and Nicodemus had provided the embalming spices. They had made it possible to bury Jesus like a king, even though He had been executed among criminals. But that didn't ease the pain much. Jesus was dead! And the saddest Sabbath in history had begun.

Sunday morning, just as it began to grow light, Mary Magdalene and some of the other women went to Jesus' tomb. But it was empty. Confused and heartbroken, Mary stood there, shuddering. All sorts of horrible thoughts deluged her mind as to what might have happened to His body. She began to cry uncontrollably, when suddenly Someone stood beside her. "Why are you crying?" He asked her tenderly. "Who is it you are looking for?" She was so upset she didn't even recognize Him but thought He was the gardener.

"Oh, sir, if you have carried Him away, please tell me where you have laid Him, and I will take Him away." Being able to care for His body was the least she could do.

Gently He said, "Mary"—quietly implying, "Mary, it's I. Don't you know who I am?"

Instantly she recognized His voice. Whirling around, she cried out His name in delight. "Master!" Jesus had repaid her love by letting her, a woman, be the first one to see Him after His death. Mary got to see Jesus even before God did.

But there was more. The angels gave Mary His message: "Tell His disciples, and Peter, that He will be in

Galilee before you. You will see Him there." *And Peter.* Since he had denied Jesus that fateful Thursday night he had lived in sheer agony. In fact, he had even contemplated suicide. He couldn't bear the thought that he had made the last few hours of Jesus' life more difficult, that he had contributed to breaking His heart. Could Jesus possibly forgive him for what he had done to Him? Would he be forever ostracized from that inner circle? The mental torture of the past few days had been almost too much for him. Those words, "And Peter" greatly comforted him, for it was Jesus' subtle way of letting him know he was forgiven, that God had accepted his repentance. The remorse Peter had gone through concerned Jesus, and rather than dwelling on all the wrong Peter had done to Him, He reached out and touched his troubled spirit.

But Jesus' invitation to Galilee involved more than just Peter. It is significant to me that Jesus was willing to rendezvous with any of His disciples. They all had deserted Him one way or another at the cross. Yet Jesus understood their fears, their human nature, and was eager to let them know that He had not spurned them because of their earlier rejection. He *wanted* to meet them again.

And when He finally came among them, He patiently and tenderly dealt with their fear and unbelief. He showed them the scars on His hands and His feet and encouraged them to touch Him to see that He was for real. Then He went one step further. Jesus ate a piece of broiled fish and some honeycomb to prove His physicalness. Instead of denouncing their lack of faith, their unbelief, He went to any length to make it easier for them to believe, to satisfy their curiosity and silence their fears.

A little later He dealt with doubting Thomas the same

way. He even allowed Thomas to touch and see the wound in His side, an intensely personal thing to do. At no time did He argue with him or put Thomas down for his pessimism. Rather, He did everything He could to dispel Thomas' doubt. He was eager for him to know that He was alive.

In the same way, today, Jesus is eager to prove His aliveness to us. And just as He was sensitive to men's needs in His time, so today He yearns to reach us with His touch of love.